Divorce, disasters, and the menopause.

Vicky Johnson

Divorce, dating, disasters, diet and menopause. © 2023 Vicky Johnson

All rights reserved.

No part of this publication may be reproduced, stored in a retrieval system, or transmitted, in any form or by any means, electronic, mechanical, photocopying, recording or otherwise, without the prior written permission of the presenters.

Vicky Johnson asserts the moral right to be identified as author of this work.

Presentation by *BookLeaf Publishing*

Web: www.bookleafpub.com

E-mail: info@bookleafpub.com

ISBN: 9789357696463

First edition 2023

DEDICATION

Sofia and luis. Always.

ACKNOWLEDGEMENT

Parents
Kids
Dog
And really good friends, who still loved me when I was absolutely miserable.

PREFACE

I'm not a writer, but I would like to be. So when I saw this challenge I thought why not. Every morning I would give myself some time , almost like a ritual to think and express. It became my diary.

menopause

Hot sweats,
Forgetfulness,
What did I enter this room to do,
Stomach bloated,
Brain fog,
My life in the menopause,
HRT,
More FML,
But it's my reality,
Give me a cuppa tea.
Did I take my medication, send that email,
where are my glasses.
Help, I'm in my mid life crisis.

Helplessness

Daily chores, daily living, numbness for feeling.
Medication, higher dose . Sleep comes and goes.
One day strong. The next weak.
 Feels helpless and meak

Dating

Nice person, no thanks. Abit edgy I'd like that.
Blocked, dating fails. Who else prevails.
Can't be bothered anymore. Help I'm swiping again

Dogs

Dog my love, sleepy head next to mine, your love is divine. Simple and no drama. I love you , you love me. It's easy.

Kids

Not friends but little humans I created, your joy and face are amazing. I love being with you. It's pure. But sometimes a battle can occur.
To watching films, eating pizza, your smiles and laughter keep me fulfilled. I simply love you. I'm alive for you. I keep healthy to watch you grow. Nothing can disappoint me from you.

divorce

Divorce. Not nice. What a life.
I will keep quiet about the things that happened,
but one day my voice will shine.

Hair

My hair is too thick. I'd like it smooth. My legs are too fat, hope they become skinny soon. My asthma is annoying, it makes me snore loud. But people say I beautiful. I don't see that, I see a confused girl.

Mental health

I think I've suffered enough, and I'd like to be just loved.
People say I'm kind, and they like me. I feel I'm never enough.
I don't know how to change this pattern. Justice in everything I've been though is a start.
 I don't think I'm ill, I had years of abuse. I hope to be better soon. And to hear the words. Your so lovely. Vicky J. You.

Toast

No money, working hard. Always a bill, to clear
.The fridge empty. Hungry stomachs. I get food
the child want. But nothing for myself. I live on
toast, usually peanut butter. It's yum.

Texting

There's one guy I like, I think he likes me too. What will happen I don't know. I'd like to have someone to do things with. I feel lonely on my own. We text a lot. It's fun. He makes me smile, and maybe he's the one.
 But knowing my luck.

Friends

Some friends are loyal. Stand with me and text me lots. Others I hear nothing from. Sometimes I feel I can't keep up, with the lunches and dinner dates. I don't care about these things. And need to be with people who relate. Who have suffered. And are in pain, need healing, and drink wine and sing in the rain. Not superficial lunches, where they don't really care. Please. No more

Hazel

I think your cold out there alone, I miss your face and yappy bark. You completely loved me. And was so loyal. Your flowers on your grave grow beautifully. Just like you my girl. My little fatty, who loved her food. Hazel I miss you. And where does my love now go? I talk to you every day. I'm glad your close. I promise Id never leave you and go away. Rest easy beautiful dog. You where the best. And loved my hazel chops.

Parents

God there the best. Worrisome daughter and grandkids. But they know we are good. I do love my parents. Very loyal and great values. Which I try and install. I hope my kids look at me like this one day. And feel I did them proud.

Future

I'd like a happy future, I see me wanting to smile again. Laughing and being relaxed, feeling the security of being ok.
I miss that about me. I was a happy child. Where does it change and you don't see that in yourself anymore.

Peace

I look for peace in everything. The flowers ,
woods, trees blowing. Music. I feel a sense
inside me to be peaceful and live a life carefree.
My dog penny is peaceful , she's a happy soul. I
want that life too.

Changes

I sense change is coming. Illness and divorce. I hope 2023 brings me something that makes sense. The changes are drastic , but liveable. And I feel we will eventually all be happy. But not yet. There's too much , so for now we live in the hope for the future .

Luis

You are simply the best thing that's ever happened to me. Bringing you up and raising you was simply the biggest honour to me. Your smiled so much as a child and was always happy. I hope you carry on and when you have children you spend quality time with then. You are adored and you adore your Oma and penny. And my son, you are simply amazing.

Sofia

My little drama queen. This will never change. You are beautiful inside and out. And remember this quality. Having a daughter, I thought we could be besties. And I'm thankful everyday for you and being your mummy. You will always be strong, and when your not I'm here. I've got you in every aspect sweetie. I absolutely adore you. And remember to wash your hair. It's just likes mummy's.

Ingram Content Group UK Ltd.
Milton Keynes UK
UKHW021847140623
423431UK00015B/369